From $20 to Millions

How Ordinary Friends Created Extraordinary Wealth with $20 a Day

JUSTICE S.M. PROSPERITY

Preface

This book was born out of a simple idea—and a bold decision. What if we could save just $20 a day? That was the question we asked ourselves. Not because we had a lot of money. Not because we had financial degrees or connections. But because we were tired of watching time pass us by while waiting for the "perfect" conditions to build wealth. We didn't start with much. Just a few friends, a common vision, and a commitment to do something extraordinary with something small. Day by day, dollar by dollar, decision by decision—we built something that would change our lives forever.We wrote *From $20 to Millions* not to impress you, but to empower you. We wanted to document our journey in a way that makes it real, practical, and repeatable. We wanted to show you that wealth isn't about luck—it's about discipline. It's not about how much you start with—it's about what you do with what you have.In these pages, you'll find more than numbers and strategies. You'll find lessons forged in real life. Stories of setbacks and comebacks. You'll see how equity, vision, prayer, and teamwork can turn an ordinary life into an extraordinary lega cy.Whether you're working a 9-to-5, juggling side hustles, or starting from scratch—this book is for you. It's a blueprint for the underdog. A field guide for dreamers. A reminder that it doesn't take millions to start—but starting can take you to millions.So wherever you are in your journey, start today. Start small. Start together.Because $20 a day might not change your life overnight—but over time, it can change everything.— Justice S. M. Prosperity

Foreword

When you hear that six people saved $20 a day and ended up building a real estate portfolio worth millions, you might be tempted to ask, "What's the catch?"But as I came to understand their story, I realized—there is no catch. No shortcuts. No secret handshakes. Just commitment, consistency, and community. This book, *From $20 to Millions*, is a powerful reminder that extraordinary wealth doesn't start with money—it starts with mindset.In a world filled with instant gratification and flashy success stories, this book stands out because it returns us to the basics: daily discipline, faith in the process, and the power of small beginnings. It's not just a financial how-to; it's a motivational movement in print.These six friends didn't come from wealth. They didn't wait for a windfall. They didn't try to time the market. Instead, they leaned into each other, committed to a simple plan, and let time and teamwork do the rest. That's what makes this story not only credible—but deeply inspiring.What you'll find in these pages is a roadmap. Not just to financial prosperity, but to personal empowerment. It's for anyone who's ever said:- "I don't have enough to start."- "The market's too crazy right now."- "Maybe one day, when things settle down."This book says, "Start now. Start small. And watch what happens when you stay faithful."Whether you're new to investing, rebuilding your finances, or simply ready to stop waiting and start doing—*From $20 to Millions* will show you what's possible.Because the truth is, wealth isn't reserved for the elite. It's available to the faithful, the focused, and the consistent.This book isn't just a story. It's a challenge. An invitation. A spark.Read it. Live it. Share it.And remember: with faith, strategy, and $20 a day—you're never starting from nothing.— Dr. Benjamin Carter, Financial Strategist & Real Estate Wealth Coach

Reader Testimonials

"I used to think you needed six figures or a miracle to start investing. This book showed me it just takes consistency, vision, and $20 a day. I'm on my second rental property now!"

— Rachel M., Nurse and first-time investor

"I've read dozens of finance books, but this one hit different. It combined strategy, spiritual truth, and real-world action steps. It gave me faith and a financial plan in the same breath."

— Darrell A., Pastor and community leader

"What makes this book special is the transparency. The wins. The mistakes. The faith. You walk away believing you can do this—and you actually can."

— Veronica T., Single mom and entrepreneur

"From $20 to Millions is more than a book—it's a blueprint. I'm leading a small group using it as a financial discipleship guide. It's changing lives."

— Marcus J., Men's ministry leader and investor

"This book broke the chains of poverty in my thinking. I used to fear money. Now I see it as a tool, a blessing, and a responsibility."

— LaToya W., Educator and youth mentor

"It's not just about real estate. It's about reclaiming your mindset and your mission. I felt like this book was written for people like me—ordinary, overlooked, and ready to rise."

— Kevin D., Warehouse worker and future landlord

"As someone who's prayed for financial breakthrough for years, this book gave me clarity and courage. It's practical, spiritual, and exactly what I needed."

— Esther O., Faith-driven entrepreneur

About the Author

Justice S.M. Prosperity (Bsc, MS, MHA, MBA, DBA(c),PTP) isn't just a name—it's a calling. A dynamic speaker, visionary entrepreneur, ordained minister, and transformative voice in financial empowerment, Justice has dedicated his life to equipping others to rise, rebuild, and rule in times of economic challenge. Blending faith and finance, his message resonates in both boardrooms and pulpits, inspiring everyday people to unlock uncommon success through practical wisdom and divine purpose.

With over 10 years of experience as a finance expert and business strategist, Justice has advised corporations, small businesses, and families on navigating economic storms with resilience and clarity. From restructuring global supply chains to guiding investors through market volatility, his insights are both time-tested and trailblazing.

Justice is the founder and CEO of Tax and Bookkeeping Done Right LLC, where he empowers clients to master their finances, minimize tax burdens, and maximize generational wealth. His powerful blend of financial literacy and spiritual insight has earned him the title "The Financial Apostle"—a bridge between biblical truth and modern wealth-building principles.

He holds three master's degrees—including Mechanical Engineering from Tuskegee University, a master's in health administration from St. Joseph's University, and an MBA in Finance from Fayetteville State University. Currently completing his Ph.D. in Business Administration at

Liberty University, Justice exemplifies the pursuit of lifelong learning and excellence.

As a sought-after speaker at national conferences and corporate events, he delivers electrifying presentations on personal finance, strategic investing, and wealth preservation. His bestselling books—*Answers to Your Money Problems, This Book Will Make You Rich, Tariffs, Trade Wars, Stock Market Meltdown, Tariffs, Trade Wars and Your* Wallet —have transformed lives by revealing secrets schools and churches too often overlook.

But beyond credentials and accolades, Justice speaks from lived experience. As a father, investor, and business leader, he's weathered economic uncertainty with unshakable faith—and emerged stronger. His strategies are not just theoretical—they're proven pathways forged in the fires of real-world challenges.

Through this book, Justice continues his divine mission: to awaken destinies, dismantle financial bondage, and ignite a new generation of leaders who prosper with purpose, power, and peace.

True wealth, he teaches, begins with wisdom. Abundance flows through faith. And success—real, lasting success—is the fruit of living with divine intention.

Prayer and Spiritual Wareface

In the pursuit of wealth, strategy is essential—but spiritual authority is irreplaceable. Many people create financial plans, set goals, and invest wisely, yet remain stuck, burdened, or blocked. Why? Because not all limitations are physical. Some are spiritual. And if you want to build lasting wealth, you must learn to pray with power, war with wisdom, and break free from the chains that seek to sabotage your progress.

The Power of Prayer in Wealth Building

Prayer is not just a religious ritual—it is a direct line to the One who owns it all."But remember the LORD your God, for it is He who gives you the power to produce wealth." — Deuteronomy 8:18 (NIV)Prayer is where clarity is born, fear is broken, and faith is fueled. Every major step in our real estate journey—every property, every decision—was bathed in prayer. Before investing, we sought wisdom. When fear tried to grip us, we declared God's promises. When a deal felt off, we paused and prayed. And time and time again, divine direction saved us from disaster and led us into favor.

Action Step: Dedicate your investment journey to God. Don't just pray for profit—pray for purpose. Ask for divine strategies, spiritual sensitivity, and supernatural provision.

Spiritual Warfare: Fighting What You Can't See

Wealth isn't just built in the bank—it's battled for in the spirit.There is a very real enemy who hates prosperity, especially the kind that glorifies

God. He would rather keep you in fear, debt, confusion, and cycles of lack. That's why the moment you decide to break generational poverty, resistance will rise. Unexpected bills. Doubt. Conflict. Confusion. But don't retreat—war wisely."For the weapons of our warfare are not carnal but mighty in God for pulling down strongholds." — 2 Corinthians 10:4 (NKJV)Declare God's word over your finances. Rebuke fear. Renounce poverty mindsets. Break generational curses in Jesus' name. When we started praying not just for money, but against the forces opposing our prosperity, we saw breakthroughs we couldn't explain with numbers alone.

Action Step: Pray offensively. Bind the spirit of fear, lack, and confusion. Loose the spirit of wisdom, favor, and provision. Make declarations like:- "I am blessed and cannot be cursed."- "I walk in divine abundance and overflow."- "Every assignment of poverty is broken in Jesus' name."

Deliverance: Breaking Free from Financial Bondage

Deliverance isn't just for the demon-possessed. It's for the bound. And many people are financially bound—not by the economy, but by inner vows, soul ties, shame, or spiritual oppression.Maybe you grew up hearing "We'll never afford that," or "People like us don't get ahead." Those words become seeds. And seeds become cycles. Deliverance is God's way of uprooting lies and setting you free."Whom the Son sets free is free indeed." — John 8:36Deliverance set us free from fear, from shame about our past financial mistakes, from guilt over wanting more, and from believing we weren't "worthy" of wealth. When God delivers you, you stop playing small. You stop surviving. And you start building—boldly.

Action Step: Ask God to show you any internal or spiritual blocks to wealth. Repent of past agreements with lack. Renounce every lie. Invite the Holy Spirit to cleanse and restore your mindset.

Combining the Spiritual and Strategic

It's not either/or—it's both. You don't have to choose between faith and financial wisdom. You were created to walk in both.Pray hard and invest smart. Break strongholds and run the numbers. Ask God for discernment and read the market. Be led by the Spirit, but know your spreadsheets.Bec ause wealth isn't just about numbers—it's about alignment. When heaven backs your hustle, your results are multiplied.

Daily Declaration for Faith-Fueled Prosperity

"Father, thank You for giving me the power to create wealth. I break every curse of poverty, fear, and limitation in Jesus' name. I declare that I am a faithful steward, a kingdom builder, and a wealth distributor. I walk in divine wisdom, favor, and overflow. What I touch prospers. I am aligned with heaven's economy. And I receive my inheritance, by faith, in full. In Jesus' name. Amen."

Contents

Chapter 1
Introduction

The $20 Decision

We didn't start with wealth. We started with faith, a few close friends, and $20 a day. This book is not about a get-rich-quick scheme. It's about a get-started-now mindset. It's about what happens when ordinary people stop waiting, start moving, and commit to something greater than themselves—one small step at a time. It began with a simple question: What if we each saved $20 a day? That's $600 a month. Over $7,000 a year. And when combined with vision, wisdom, and unity—it became the seed of a real estate journey that would change everything. At first, we had doubts. We asked ourselves:- Is this even enough to make a difference?- Can six regular people really build wealth like the pros?- What if we fail? But then we asked a better question. What if it works? And it did. Not because we were lucky, but because we were faithful. Faithful to the daily habit. Faithful to the process. Faithful to the dream we carried together. In these pages, you'll find the exact blueprint we used—how we went from saving small amounts to acquiring multiple rental properties, leveraging equity, and growing our net worth year after year. You'll see our mistakes, our lessons, and our victories. You'll get charts, projections, and step-by-step strategies. But more than that, you'll get hope. Because the world needs fewer theories and more testimonies. And this book is a testimony to what's possible when you move in faith and act in wisdom.

This is for the underdog. For the dreamer who's ready to act. For the everyday person who's tired of being stuck and ready to build something lasting. You don't need millions to start. You need a vision. You need a community. And you need $20 a day. Let's begin.

Chapter 2

The Journey Begins

Understanding the $20 Daily Challenge

Understanding the $20 Daily Challenge is the first step towards transforming your financial future through real estate investment. By committing to save just $20 each day, you and your partner can accumulate significant resources over time. This challenge is not just about saving; it's about fostering a mindset geared towards wealth creation. With six individuals, including three couples, pooling their efforts, the savings quickly add up. In just one year, each couple can contribute nearly $14,600, setting the stage for the annual purchase of rental properties that can generate passive income and build equity.

The strategy is simple yet powerful: every year, the group can utilize 7% of a home's price, which is approximately $14,000 for a $200,000 property, as a down payment. By working together, couples can leverage their collective savings to make real estate investments that would be difficult to achieve alone. This collaborative approach not only amplifies each couple's financial power but also strengthens relationships through shared goals and teamwork. The sense of unity and commitment to a common vision can enhance both financial and personal bonds within the group.

As the years pass, the power of the $20 Daily Challenge becomes even more evident. After five years of consistent saving and investing, the group will have acquired multiple properties, each contributing to their overall wealth. By year six, they can tap into the accumulated home equity of their initial investments to fund further down payments. This strategy allows them to reinvest in new properties without depleting their daily savings, creating a cycle of growth that accelerates their journey towards building a robust rental portfolio.

Long-term planning is crucial in this endeavor. The goal is not just to buy properties but to establish a sustainable investment strategy that continues to grow over 10 to 15 years. Each property acquired adds to the group's income and increases their potential for future investments. By embracing daily savings habits, the couples can cultivate a disciplined approach to financial management that pays off significantly in the long run. This commitment to saving and investing lays a solid foundation for future financial stability and wealth accumulation.

The $20 Daily Challenge embodies a spirit of collaboration, encouraging couples to work together towards a shared financial goal. By engaging in this challenge, participants not only improve their financial literacy but also enhance their relationship dynamics. The challenge fosters open discussions about money, encourages joint decision-making, and nurtures a sense of collective responsibility. Through strategic planning and commitment, the group can achieve their dream of property ownership while enjoying the journey of building a successful real estate investment portfolio together.

The Power of Collective Savings

The power of collective savings can transform financial dreams into reality, especially when it comes to property investment. Imagine a group of six individuals, three couples, each committing to save just $20 a day. Over the course of a year, their combined effort results in a staggering $43,800, enough to make a significant impact in the real estate market. By pooling their savings, these couples not only increase their purchasing power but also foster a supportive environment that encourages accountability and shared financial goals. This collaborative effort can serve as a powerful motivator, helping each individual stay committed to their savings journey.

As the couples begin to save and strategize together, they can set clear goals on how to utilize their combined funds. With the target of purchasing rental properties, they can allocate 7% of a home priced at $200,000 as a down payment, which amounts to $14,000. By pooling their savings, they can easily cover this cost, opening the door to property ownership. The excitement of owning rental properties not only provides a sense of accomplishment but also sets the stage for long-term financial growth. This shared vision can strengthen their relationships and enhance their collective commitment to financial stability.

The strategy is not just about saving; it's about establishing a long-term plan that maximizes their investment potential. Over the next 10 to 15 years, these couples can aim to purchase one or two houses annually, steadily building a robust rental portfolio. Each property acquired adds to their financial foundation, creating opportunities for passive income and capital appreciation. The discipline of daily savings, when applied collectively, can lead to incredible results and instill a sense of pride in their journey toward financial independence.

Starting in year six, the couples can leverage the equity from their first five properties to fund down payments for additional investments. This strategy not only accelerates their property acquisition but also exemplifies the power of using existing assets to create new opportunities. As they continue to grow their portfolio, they will learn valuable lessons about property management, market trends, and investment strategies, which can further enhance their financial acumen and confidence in real estate.

Ultimately, the collective savings approach fosters a sense of community and shared purpose among the couples. By working together, they can navigate the complexities of real estate investment while also enjoying the benefits of mutual support and encouragement. This journey is not just about building wealth; it's about creating lasting connections and empowering each other to achieve dreams that may initially seem unattainable. Embracing the power of collective savings can truly transform their financial futures while paving the way for a thriving rental property portfolio.

Meeting Our Couples: Diverse Backgrounds, Shared Goals

In the journey of financial empowerment, the stories of couples from diverse backgrounds come together in a powerful narrative. Each couple brings unique experiences and perspectives that enrich their shared mission of saving $20 a day. They might be young professionals, newlyweds, or long-term partners; what unites them is a commitment to transform their savings into property ownership. This common goal fosters a sense of camaraderie and collaboration that transcends their individual differences, illustrating that when people unite over a shared ambition, they can achieve remarkable outcomes.

Consider Alex and Jamie, who hail from different cities but found each other in a bustling urban community. With Alex's analytical mindset and Jamie's creativity, they make the perfect team. They meticulously track their savings, turning the daily act of saving into a fun challenge. They celebrate small wins together, whether it's reaching a milestone in their savings or completing a successful property acquisition. Their approach not only strengthens their financial stability but also deepens their relationship as they work toward a common goal.

Then there's Chris and Taylor, both passionate about sustainability. They are keen on investing in properties that not only provide financial returns but also contribute positively to the community. Their focus on environmentally friendly renovations and energy-efficient homes allows them to align their values with their investment strategy. By pooling their resources with others, they amplify their impact, proving that real estate investment can be both profitable and purposeful. Their journey demonstrates that shared values can enhance collaboration and make the path to property ownership even more rewarding.

The third couple, Sam and Jordan, represent a blend of different cultures, each bringing their family's traditions and financial philosophies into their partnership. This diversity enriches their discussions around savings techniques and investment strategies. They actively share insights from their backgrounds, learning from each other's approaches to money management. As they navigate the complexities of real estate investment, they realize that their diverse experiences make them stronger as a unit, allowing them to develop innovative strategies for property acquisition that incorporate various perspectives.

Together, these couples exemplify the power of teamwork in the realm of real estate investment. By committing to save $20 each day and pooling their annual savings for down payments, they are not just building a portfolio of rental properties; they are also constructing a community of support and encouragement. Their stories inspire others who may feel overwhelmed by the prospect of property investment, showing that with dedication, strategic planning, and shared goals, anyone can embark on a successful journey toward financial independence through real estate. As they move forward, they embody the belief that success is not just measured by financial gain but also by the relationships and experiences nurtured along the way.

Chapter 3

Laying the Foundation

The Importance of Financial Literacy

Financial literacy is a crucial skill that empowers individuals, especially beginners, to take control of their financial futures. Understanding the basic principles of finance is essential for anyone embarking on the journey of property investment. For the couples participating in the $20 Daily Challenge, financial literacy will not only enhance their ability to save but also enable them to make informed decisions about real estate investments. Knowing how to budget, track expenses, and understand the implications of debt can significantly impact the success of their collective goals.

As these couples commit to saving $20 a day, they will soon realize that knowledge is their strongest asset. Financial literacy helps them understand the importance of compound interest and how their daily savings can grow over time. By pooling their resources, they can harness the power of collective savings, which will ultimately lead to substantial down payments for rental properties. This teamwork, underpinned by a solid understanding of financial concepts, will foster a sense of unity and purpose among them, making the journey enjoyable and rewarding.

Moreover, being financially literate will allow these couples to identify and evaluate potential investment opportunities effectively. As they aim to purchase rental properties, they will encounter various financial metrics and terms that can seem daunting at first. With a foundational understanding of concepts such as cash flow, return on investment, and equity, they can make strategic decisions about which properties to buy and when to leverage their growing equity. This knowledge will not only assist them in making wise choices but also instill confidence in their investment strategies.

The importance of financial literacy extends beyond just understanding numbers; it also encompasses the ability to communicate and collaborate effectively. For couples investing together, discussing financial goals and strategies is vital. By fostering an environment where financial topics are openly discussed, they can navigate challenges and celebrate successes as a team. This collaborative approach will strengthen their relationship while ensuring that both partners are aligned in their investment journey, ultimately leading to a more successful property portfolio.

Lastly, as these couples progress in their journey, their financial literacy will inspire others in their communities. By sharing their experiences and knowledge, they become role models for other aspiring investors, particularly young individuals who may feel overwhelmed by the prospect of investing in real estate. Their commitment to ongoing education and growth will not only benefit their own financial futures but will also encourage a culture of financial literacy that can transform the lives of many. Through this journey, they will learn that knowledge, when combined with disciplined saving and strategic investing, can lead to remarkable financial freedom.

Setting Up a Savings Plan

Setting up a savings plan is a vital first step for anyone looking to transform their financial future through real estate. For our group of six individuals—three couples—committing to save $20 a day each, the process begins with setting clear, achievable goals. Each member should take some time to identify personal financial objectives, such as how much they want to save by the end of the year and what type of properties they are interested in purchasing. Establishing these goals not only provides a sense of purpose but also fosters accountability within the group, as everyone works towards a shared vision of building a rental portfolio together.

Next, it's essential to create a structured savings plan that outlines how the group will pool their daily contributions. By saving $20 each day, each couple will contribute $40 daily, totaling $240 per day for the group. Over a year, this amounts to approximately $87,600. Setting up a dedicated savings account for this pooled fund can help keep the savings organized and separate from personal expenses. This account should ideally offer some interest, allowing the money to grow gradually while the group prepares for property acquisitions. Regular meetings to review progress can keep everyone motivated and ensure that everyone is on track with their contributions.

To optimize the savings strategy, consider automating the contributions. Setting up automatic transfers to the joint savings account ensures that the $240 is saved every day without requiring manual intervention. Automating savings not only simplifies the process but also reinforces the habit of saving, making it easier for each couple to reach their financial goals. Additionally, small adjustments in daily spending habits can contribute significantly to the savings plan. Encouraging each couple to identify areas where they can cut back—like dining out less or forgoing certain subscriptions—can help boost their daily savings without a significant lifestyle change.

As the group progresses and begins to see their savings accumulate, it's important to educate themselves about the real estate market. Understanding property values, rental income potential, and market trends will empower the group to make informed decisions when it comes time to purchase their first property. Engaging in discussions about investment strategies and pooling knowledge can create a collaborative environment where everyone benefits from shared insights. This collective learning experience not only strengthens the group dynamic but also enhances their ability to navigate the complexities of real estate investment together.

Finally, as they approach the sixth year and begin to leverage the equity from their first properties, it's crucial to reassess and refine their savings plan. The ability to use 7% of the home price as a down payment for subsequent purchases will allow the group to accelerate their portfolio growth. Regularly revisiting their financial goals and adapting their strategies will ensure that they remain aligned with their vision of building a robust rental portfolio. By maintaining a strong commitment to their daily savings habit and supporting each other through the journey, they can transform their initial $20 daily challenge into a thriving real estate investment venture that provides lasting financial security.

Creating a Budget that Works

Creating a budget that works is essential for anyone embarking on the journey of real estate investment, especially for couples and groups pooling their resources. The first step in crafting a successful budget is to assess your current financial situation. Gather all relevant income and expense information, and categorize them into fixed costs, variable expenses, and discretionary spending. Understanding where your money goes each month will empower you to identify areas where you can cut back and save the $20 daily. This awareness will not only strengthen your commitment but also foster a team spirit among your group as you collectively work towards a shared goal.

Next, set clear and achievable savings goals. In this case, each couple should aim to save $600 a month, which adds up to $7,200 annually per couple. As you pool these savings, the collective power of your group becomes apparent. Make it a fun challenge to find ways to reach these savings goals. Consider implementing a friendly competition among couples to see who can find the most creative ways to save money. This camaraderie not only makes budgeting enjoyable but also keeps everyone motivated to stick to their financial commitments.

Once you have a clear savings goal, it's time to create a detailed budget that aligns with your group's objectives. Include all necessary expenses but ensure that your savings goal is a non-negotiable line item in the budget. Use budgeting apps or spreadsheets to track your spending in real-time, allowing you to adjust as needed. The key is to remain flexible; if one month you go over budget in one category, find a way to compensate in another. This adaptability will help maintain morale and keep everyone focused on the long-term vision of acquiring rental properties.

Incorporating daily savings habits into your routine can also help solidify your budgeting strategy. Encourage each couple to automate their $20 contributions to a dedicated savings account. Setting up automatic transfers to your investment fund removes the temptation to spend that money elsewhere. Consider designating one day each week as "Savings Sunday," where you all gather to review progress, discuss challenges, and celebrate milestones. This regular check-in will reinforce your commitment and allow for continued collaboration on financial strategies.

Finally, as you progress towards your first property purchase, regularly revisit and adjust your budget. As your group dynamics evolve and your financial situation changes, it's crucial to ensure your budgeting plan remains relevant. Engage in open conversations about financial goals and any challenges that may arise. Remember, the journey of real estate investment is a marathon, not a sprint. By fostering a supportive environment and maintaining a well-structured budget, you will not only achieve your goal of acquiring rental properties but also build lasting financial habits that benefit each couple in the long run.

Chapter 4
The Art of Saving
Daily Habits that Fuel Savings

Daily habits play a crucial role in fueling savings and setting the foundation for successful property investments. For couples embarking on the journey of pooling resources to save $20 daily, establishing consistent behaviors can make all the difference in achieving long-term financial goals. By embracing small yet impactful daily practices, you can cultivate a mindset geared toward saving and investing. This chapter will explore effective habits that can enhance your journey towards acquiring rental properties, ensuring that your collective efforts translate into tangible results.

One effective daily habit is to track your expenses diligently. By recording every purchase, no matter how small, you create awareness of your spending patterns. This practice can reveal areas where you might be overspending and help identify opportunities for saving. Encourage each other to review your daily expenditures and discuss ways to cut back on non-essential items. For instance, choosing to cook at home instead of dining out can save significant amounts over time. When you collectively commit to being mindful of your spending, you reinforce your shared goal of saving for real estate.

Another powerful habit is to set daily savings reminders. Use technology to your advantage by setting up alerts on your phone or calendar to remind you to save that $20 each day. This simple act can transform saving from an afterthought into a priority. Additionally, consider creating a visual savings tracker that you can display prominently in your home. Watching your savings grow, even if it's just a small amount each day, can provide motivation and a sense of accomplishment, making the journey toward property ownership feel tangible and achievable.

Incorporating a daily routine that includes financial education can also be beneficial. Allocate a specific time each day to read articles, watch videos, or listen to podcasts about real estate investing and personal finance. By expanding your knowledge together, you not only strengthen your financial literacy but also nurture a collaborative approach to investment strategies. Learning about market trends, property management, and financing options will empower you as a couple, making you more equipped to make informed decisions as you build your rental portfolio.

Lastly, fostering open communication about finances is essential. Make it a habit to discuss your financial goals and progress regularly. Set aside time each week to sit down together and review your savings, discuss any challenges you've encountered, and celebrate your milestones. This practice not only keeps both partners aligned and motivated but also reinforces the commitment to your shared vision of property ownership. The more you communicate and collaborate, the stronger your partnership will become, ultimately enhancing your collective investment journey.

By integrating these daily habits into your routine, you create a supportive environment conducive to saving and investing in real estate. Embrace the power of small, consistent actions and watch as they compound over time, leading to significant progress towards your goal of building a robust rental portfolio. Remember, every dollar saved brings you one step closer to making your property investment dreams a reality, and with dedication and teamwork, you can achieve financial success together.

Overcoming Financial Obstacles

Overcoming financial obstacles is a journey that begins with commitment and determination. For the six individuals embarking on the $20 Daily Challenge, the first step is to shift their mindset from scarcity to abundance. This transformation is crucial, as it allows each participant to view their $20 daily savings not as a sacrifice but as an investment in their future. By pooling their resources, these couples create a powerful collective force that amplifies their savings potential and accelerates their path toward property ownership.

The beauty of the $20 Daily Challenge lies in its simplicity. Each member saves just $20 a day, which may seem insignificant at first glance. However, over the course of a year, this amounts to a substantial sum when combined. Together, the couples can save over $43,000 annually. This collaborative approach not only strengthens their financial position but also fosters a sense of accountability and teamwork. By encouraging one another and celebrating small milestones along the way, they build a supportive environment that helps everyone stay focused on their shared goal of acquiring rental properties.

As they navigate the financial landscape, challenges will inevitably arise. Unexpected expenses, changes in income, or even shifts in personal priorities can pose hurdles. However, by adopting proactive savings techniques, the couples can better prepare for these obstacles. Establishing an emergency fund, for instance, can provide a financial cushion that allows them to stay on track. Additionally, they can explore creative ways to cut expenses, from meal planning to finding new sources of income, ensuring that their $20 daily commitment remains unwavering.

In the later years of their investment journey, the couples will begin to leverage the equity built in their properties to fund further acquisitions. This strategy requires careful financial planning and a keen understanding of market trends. By educating themselves about property values and investment strategies, they can make informed decisions that maximize their returns. The collaborative nature of their investment group will prove invaluable here, as each couple brings unique insights and experiences to the table, enriching the decision-making process.

Ultimately, the key to overcoming financial obstacles lies in persistence and adaptability. The couples must remain focused on their long-term goals while being flexible enough to adjust their strategies as needed. By maintaining a daily savings habit and fostering a culture of support, they will not only achieve their desired outcome of building a robust rental portfolio but will also develop skills and resilience that extend beyond real estate. The journey may be challenging, but with dedication and teamwork, they can turn their dreams into reality, proving that financial success is indeed within reach.

Tools and Apps for Tracking Savings

In the journey to transform savings into property, utilizing tools and apps for tracking your savings can make a significant difference. For beginners, especially those who are part of a collaborative group like the six individuals pooling their daily savings, having an effective system in place is essential. There are numerous apps designed specifically for budgeting and savings that can help you stay on track with your daily $20 savings challenge. These tools not only allow you to monitor your progress but also offer insights into your spending habits, which can be invaluable as you work toward your property acquisition goals.

One popular app that many find useful is Mint. This app connects to your bank accounts, automatically categorizing your transactions and providing a clear picture of your financial landscape. For couples or groups, it allows you to set collective savings goals, track contributions, and celebrate milestones together. By visualizing your progress toward the down payment for your first rental property, you can maintain motivation and accountability, ensuring that everyone remains committed to the collective goal.

Another excellent tool is YNAB (You Need A Budget), which is particularly effective for those new to budgeting. YNAB helps you allocate every dollar to specific categories, encouraging users to prioritize savings. This proactive approach is ideal for groups aiming to save a significant amount each year. By adopting YNAB, couples can work together to create a spending plan that aligns with their long-term investment strategy, ensuring that the $20 saved each day is consistently contributing to the down payment fund.

For those who prefer a more visual approach, digital savings jars or envelope systems can be incredibly motivating. Apps like Qapital allow users to set specific savings goals and automate contributions based on rules you define. For instance, you could set a rule that rounds up your purchases to the nearest dollar, with the extra cents going straight into your savings jar for the down payment. This gamification of savings can be especially appealing for youth and beginners, making the process of saving both fun and rewarding.

Lastly, don't underestimate the power of simple spreadsheets or budgeting templates. These tools can help track daily savings and visualize your journey toward property ownership. By updating your spreadsheet regularly, you can see your savings grow, making it easier to stay focused on your goals. Whether you choose a high-tech app or a straightforward spreadsheet, the key is to find a system that works for your group dynamic. By staying organized and committed, you'll be well on your way to building a robust rental portfolio together, turning your daily savings into valuable properties over the years.

Chapter 5

Group Dynamics in Investment

Building Trust and Communication

Building trust and communication among group members is crucial for the success of your collective real estate investment journey. As you embark on this exciting path with your partners, establishing a strong foundation of trust will ensure that everyone feels secure and valued in the decision-making process. Trust is built over time through consistent, open dialogue and shared experiences. Make it a priority to meet regularly, whether in person or virtually, to discuss not only your financial goals but also your challenges and successes. These meetings will foster a sense of camaraderie and commitment to the group's shared vision.

Effective communication is the lifeblood of any successful partnership, especially when dealing with finances. Encourage each member to voice their thoughts, concerns, and ideas. This open forum will help clarify expectations and minimize misunderstandings. Consider using collaborative tools like shared documents or apps where everyone can track contributions, savings progress, and property performance. This transparency not only keeps everyone informed but also reinforces accountability. Remember, the more you communicate, the stronger your collective resolve will become.

As you save $20 a day, it's essential to celebrate milestones together. Whether it's achieving your first $10,000 in savings or successfully purchasing your first property, acknowledge these achievements as a group. Celebrating these moments not only boosts morale but also strengthens the bond among partners. You might even consider hosting a small gathering or outing to commemorate each milestone. These experiences will deepen your relationships and remind everyone of the shared purpose behind your efforts.

Conflict may arise as you navigate the complexities of property investment, but viewing these moments as opportunities for growth is vital. Approach disagreements with an open mind and a willingness to listen. Encourage each member to express their views and work collaboratively to find solutions that benefit the group as a whole. By addressing conflicts constructively, you will not only resolve issues but also reinforce trust and communication within the team. Remember, it's not about winning arguments but about finding common ground and moving forward together.

Lastly, as your group grows and evolves, so will your communication dynamics. Be open to adapting your strategies and processes as needed. Regularly assess how well your communication is working and be willing to make changes to improve it. This flexibility will help you navigate the challenges of real estate investment more effectively. Embracing these principles of trust and communication will empower your group to achieve your shared goals, transforming your daily savings into a thriving rental property portfolio over the coming years.

Roles within the Group

In any group investment strategy, understanding the roles within the group is essential for fostering collaboration and achieving shared goals.

Each member brings unique strengths and perspectives, and recognizing these contributions can lead to greater success. For the six individuals in this challenge, dividing responsibilities can streamline the process of saving, investing, and managing properties. By clearly defining roles, the group can ensure that each member feels valued and engaged, which is crucial for maintaining motivation over the long term.

One important role is that of the organizer or coordinator, who takes the lead in setting up meetings, tracking savings, and keeping everyone accountable. This person can create a shared calendar to ensure that everyone is on the same page regarding their savings goals and property acquisitions. By facilitating communication, the organizer helps to foster a sense of unity within the group, making it easier for everyone to contribute their ideas and concerns. This role is particularly vital in the early stages, as the group establishes its routines and builds momentum toward their financial goals.

Another key role is the researcher or analyst, responsible for investigating potential properties and market trends. This individual can gather data on neighborhoods, rental rates, and property values, providing the group with the information needed to make informed decisions. By taking on this responsibility, the researcher empowers the group to invest wisely, ensuring that they purchase properties that will appreciate over time and generate positive cash flow. This role can also involve networking with real estate agents and other investors, expanding the group's connection to valuable resources and insights.

Financial management is another critical aspect of the group's success, and having a dedicated finance manager can make a significant difference. This person will oversee the budgeting process, ensuring that the group's daily savings of $20 each are consistently pooled and allocated toward down payments and other expenses. By keeping detailed records and tracking expenditures, the finance manager can help the group stay on budget and make adjustments as needed. This role also includes evaluating the group's overall financial health, providing regular updates on progress toward their investment goals.

Finally, the role of the motivator or cheerleader cannot be understated. This person is responsible for maintaining enthusiasm and morale throughout the journey, especially during challenging times or when the group faces obstacles. By celebrating milestones and reminding everyone of the bigger picture, the motivator plays a crucial role in keeping spirits high. With a positive mindset and encouragement, this individual can inspire the group to persevere, reinforcing the idea that their collective efforts will lead to long-term success in building a rental property portfolio. When each member embraces their role, the group can work together harmoniously, unlocking the potential for financial transformation through real estate investment.

Conflict Resolution Strategies

Conflict is a natural part of any group endeavor, especially when it comes to financial decisions and investments like real estate. When six individuals commit to a shared goal of saving $20 daily to pool resources for property purchases, differing opinions and priorities may arise. To navigate these challenges, it is essential to implement effective conflict resolution strategies that can enhance collaboration and ensure everyone remains focused on the common goal of building a successful rental portfolio.

The first strategy involves open communication. Create an environment where all group members feel comfortable expressing their thoughts and concerns. Regular meetings can facilitate discussions about individual contributions, investment choices, and any challenges that may arise. Encourage each person to share their perspective without fear of judgment. This openness fosters trust and helps to identify potential conflicts before they escalate, allowing for proactive solutions to be discussed and implemented.

Another effective approach is to establish clear roles and responsibilities within the group. By defining who does what, you can minimize misunderstandings and ensure everyone knows their contributions are valuable and appreciated. For example, assign roles based on strengths—some might focus on researching properties, while others manage finances or handle negotiations. Clarity in responsibilities helps to prevent overlap and conflict, as each member understands their specific duties and how they fit into the larger vision of the group.

When conflicts do arise, it is crucial to approach them with a problem-solving mindset rather than a confrontational one. Encourage group members to view disagreements as opportunities for growth and improvement. When faced with a conflict, take a step back and collectively analyze the situation. Ask questions like, "What is the best outcome for everyone?" or "How can we align our strategies with our shared goals?" This collaborative approach can turn potential disputes into productive discussions that strengthen the group's bond and commitment.

Lastly, celebrate successes together, no matter how small. Acknowledging achievements not only boosts morale but also reinforces the shared commitment to the group's objectives. Whether it's reaching a savings milestone or successfully purchasing a property, taking time to celebrate these moments fosters a sense of unity. It reminds everyone of the importance of teamwork and the collective effort required to achieve long-term goals. By maintaining a positive atmosphere and focusing on shared victories, you can create a resilient group dynamic that thrives on collaboration and mutual support.

By implementing these conflict resolution strategies, couples and individuals engaged in the $20 Daily Challenge can navigate challenges with confidence. Emphasizing open communication, clearly defined roles, problem-solving approaches, and celebrating successes will not only strengthen relationships but also enhance the overall effectiveness of the group. This collaborative spirit is essential in building a robust rental property portfolio that will serve everyone's financial goals for years to come.

Chapter 6
From Savings to Property

Understanding down payments

Understanding down payments is a crucial step in your journey toward property ownership, especially as a group of committed individuals pooling your savings. A down payment is the upfront amount you pay when purchasing a property, and it plays a significant role in determining your mortgage terms and monthly payments. For your goal of acquiring rental properties, a solid understanding of how down payments work can empower you to make informed decisions and maximize your collective investment strategy.

In your case, aiming to save $20 each day allows you to accumulate a substantial amount over time. If each of the six individuals in your group manages to save $20 daily, that totals $120 per day. Over a year, this adds up to $43,800. With a target home price of $200,000, a down payment of 7% amounts to $14,000. This means that within just a year, your group can easily meet the down payment requirement for a property, demonstrating the immense power of consistent savings.

As you progress through your investment journey, remember that the down payment is not just a financial hurdle; it's a pathway to building equity in your properties. Each time you purchase a new home, you're not only gaining an asset but also a source of income through rental payments. This income can be reinvested in your strategy, allowing you to buy more properties in the future and build a robust rental portfolio. The cycle of saving, buying, and reinvesting is key to accelerating your growth as a collective real estate investment group.

Starting from year six, leveraging the equity built from your initial properties can further enhance your down payment strategy. As property values increase, so does the equity you hold in those homes. This equity can be tapped into to finance new down payments, enabling you to acquire additional properties without needing to save as extensively each year. This strategic approach will keep your momentum going, allowing your group to expand its portfolio more rapidly than you initially thought possible.

Ultimately, understanding down payments is about more than just the money; it's about fostering a habit of saving, collaborating with your partners, and setting clear financial goals. Each small step you take today, like saving $20 daily, contributes to a larger vision of property ownership and financial independence. By working together and maintaining your commitment to saving, you'll not only transform your financial futures but also create lasting change in your lives and the lives of others through the rental properties you acquire.

Navigating the Real Estate Market

Navigating the real estate market can seem daunting, especially for beginners, but with a clear strategy and commitment, it becomes an exciting journey. For the six individuals in our group, who have decided to pool their daily savings of $20, the focus is on building a rental property portfolio together. This collaborative approach not only minimizes individual risk but also amplifies the potential for success. By understanding the dynamics of the real estate market, each member can play a vital role in achieving their shared goal of property ownership.

The first step in navigating the market is to familiarize yourself with the basics of real estate investing. As newbies, it's essential to learn about property values, rental rates, and market trends. By pooling resources, each couple can conduct thorough research, attend workshops, or connect with real estate professionals. This collective knowledge base will empower all members to make informed decisions when purchasing properties. Remember, staying educated about the market is a crucial aspect of successful investment.

As the group embarks on their journey, establishing a solid financial plan is vital. Saving $20 a day may seem small, but over time, it accumulates to a substantial amount. By the end of the year, each couple will contribute $7,300, which can be strategically used as a 7% down payment on a $200,000 property. This disciplined approach to saving not only builds a robust foundation but also fosters a sense of accountability among group members. As the years progress, the equity gained from their initial property purchases will allow them to leverage their investments for further acquisitions, creating a snowball effect in their portfolio growth.

One of the key advantages of group investment is the ability to tackle challenges together. Whether it's navigating the complexities of property management or identifying the right opportunities, each couple can rely on the strengths and insights of the others. Developing a collaborative mindset will enhance decision-making and problem-solving within the group. Emphasizing open communication and shared goals will keep everyone motivated and focused, helping to turn potential obstacles into stepping stones for success.

As the years pass and the group continues to invest, their long-term vision should remain clear. The goal is not just to acquire properties but to create a sustainable rental income that can support future endeavors. By implementing effective savings techniques and leveraging equity, they can accelerate their growth and potentially own multiple properties. The journey of navigating the real estate market is not just about financial gain; it's about building a legacy and achieving dreams together. With dedication and a strategic approach, the possibilities are endless.

Identifying Profitable Rental Properties

Identifying profitable rental properties is a crucial step for any group embarking on a collaborative real estate investment journey. For the six individuals in our challenge, it's not just about pooling resources but also about making informed decisions that will yield long-term financial benefits. The first step is to understand what makes a property a good investment. Look for locations experiencing growth, such as areas with new job opportunities, schools, and amenities. Researching local market trends will help you identify neighborhoods where property values are likely to appreciate, ensuring that your investment pays off over time.

Another important factor to consider is the rental yield, which is a measure of how much income a property generates relative to its purchase price. Aim for properties that can provide a rental yield of at least 8% to 10%. This means that if you purchase a $200,000 property, you should aim for rental income of $1,600 to $2,000 per month. This can give you a solid cash flow to cover expenses and reinvest in future properties. Utilize online resources and rental calculators to analyze potential rental income against property costs, enabling you to make data-driven decisions.

As a group, it's essential to leverage diverse perspectives and expertise when evaluating potential properties. Each member of your investment team may have different strengths, whether in finance, negotiation, or property management. Collaborate to conduct thorough property inspections and due diligence. This not only ensures that you are aware of any potential issues before closing the deal but also fosters team cohesion and accountability. Learning to communicate openly about each member's insights will enhance your ability to spot lucrative opportunities and avoid potential pitfalls.

Consider the long-term implications of your property choices. Investing in rental properties is not just about immediate cash flow; it's also about building a sustainable portfolio that can grow in value over time. Look for properties that have potential for renovation or improvement, allowing you to increase their value and rental income. By being proactive and creative in your approach, you can significantly enhance the profitability of your investments, setting the stage for future acquisitions and growing your real estate portfolio.

Finally, remember to stay committed to your savings plan and investment strategy. A disciplined approach to saving $20 a day may seem small, but over time, it can lead to substantial wealth creation through real estate. Celebrate your successes, learn from any setbacks, and always be on the lookout for new opportunities. By cultivating a mindset of perseverance and collaboration, you will not only identify profitable rental properties but also create a thriving investment community that empowers each member to achieve their financial goals.

Chapter 7
The First Property Purchase

Preparing for your first investment

Preparing for your first investment can be both exciting and daunting, especially when your part of a group dedicated to the same goal. As you embark on this journey with your partners, it's crucial to foster a shared understanding of your collective mission. Begin by having open conversations about your financial goals, risk tolerance, and investment strategies. This collaborative mindset will not only strengthen your relationships but will also establish a foundation of trust and mutual support. Remember, each member brings unique insights that can enhance your overall approach to saving and investing.

Establishing a solid savings plan is your first step toward successful property investment. By committing to save $20 daily, you and your partners are already setting a powerful example of discipline and dedication. Track your savings collectively, perhaps through an online tool or an app designed for group finances. This transparency will keep everyone motivated and accountable. Celebrate milestones together, like reaching your first $10,000 in savings, to maintain enthusiasm and reinforce your collective commitment to the goal.

Once you have a clear savings strategy, it's essential to educate yourselves about the real estate market. Knowledge is a powerful tool in investment, especially as first-time buyers. Attend workshops, read books, and follow real estate blogs to familiarize yourselves with market trends, property values, and investment strategies. Understanding the nuances of home buying, such as the importance of location and property management, can significantly impact your success. Make learning a group activity; discuss what you find and how it applies to your investment strategy.

As you prepare to make your first purchase, focus on the importance of leveraging your down payment effectively. With your goal of using 7% of a $200,000 home price, you'll need to work collaboratively to ensure that everyone is on track to contribute their share. Explore different financing options and potential partnerships with local banks or credit unions that may offer favorable terms for first-time investors. Researching these options together can lead to better decisions and potentially lower costs, increasing your overall return on investment.

Finally, embrace the idea of flexibility and adaptability in your investment journey. Real estate markets can be unpredictable, and unexpected challenges may arise. By maintaining open lines of communication with your partners, you can navigate these challenges together. Remember that your ultimate goal is to build a robust rental portfolio over time. Stay focused on your strategy, but be willing to pivot and adjust as needed. The commitment to saving and investing as a cohesive group will not only lead to financial success but will also foster lifelong friendships and partnerships.

The Buying Process Explained

Understanding the buying process is essential for any group of aspiring real estate investors, especially for those taking the exciting first steps like you and your partners. The journey begins with a clear commitment to save daily. Each couple in your group has decided to contribute $20 a day, which may seem modest at first glance but accumulates significantly over time. By pooling your resources, you create a powerful financial force, enabling each of you to approach property purchases with confidence. This daily habit not only builds your savings but also fosters a sense of teamwork and shared purpose among you.

Once you have amassed your savings, the next step in the buying process involves determining how much you can invest in rental properties. With a target home price of $200,000, you'll want to set aside 7% of that amount for a down payment, which translates to $14,000. By working together, you can easily reach this goal sooner than you might expect. Each year, as you continue your savings strategy, you will be able to purchase one or even two properties, expanding your portfolio and setting the stage for future growth.

As you move forward with the purchasing process, it's crucial to conduct thorough research on potential properties. Evaluate neighborhoods, property conditions, and market trends to make informed decisions. Engage in discussions with your partners about your findings and conduct property viewings together. This collaborative approach not only strengthens your collective knowledge but also ensures that everyone feels invested in the decision-making process. Remember, the more informed you are, the better choices you'll make, reducing risks and maximizing returns.

Financing your purchases is another key element of the buying process. With your initial properties secured, you'll start to see the benefits of equity growth. By year six, you'll have accumulated significant equity that can be leveraged for down payments on additional properties. This strategic use of home equity will allow you to accelerate your investment strategy and acquire more rental properties. It's a powerful tool that transforms your initial investments into a broader real estate portfolio, generating passive income and financial security.

Lastly, keep in mind that building a real estate portfolio is not just about purchasing properties; it's about nurturing your group's dynamics and maintaining open communication. Regular meetings to discuss progress, challenges, and strategies will ensure that everyone is aligned with your collective goals. Celebrate your achievements, no matter how small, and support each other through setbacks. By fostering a collaborative and encouraging environment, you will not only enhance your chances of success but also create lasting bonds that enrich your investment journey. Embrace this process, and you will be well on your way to transforming your savings into a thriving rental property empire.

Celebrating Your Success

Celebrating your success is an essential part of any journey, especially when it comes to transforming your savings into property. As you and your group of six individuals, comprising three couples, embark on this exciting venture of saving $20 a day, it's vital to take a moment to acknowledge and celebrate each milestone you achieve. Whether it's reaching your first $1,000 in savings or successfully purchasing your first rental property, each step forward represents hard work, commitment, and the promise of a brighter financial future. Celebrating these victories not only boosts morale but also reinforces the bond among your group, making your collaborative efforts even stronger.

As you pool your savings and work toward your shared goal of acquiring rental properties, recognize the importance of milestones beyond just financial targets. Celebrate the learning experiences along the way — the discussions about investment strategies, the research you conduct together, and the teamwork involved in decision-making. These moments contribute to your growth as investors and deepen your understanding of the real estate market. Each discussion, each insight gained, is a step closer to your ultimate goal, and acknowledging these moments can provide motivation to keep pushing forward.

When you achieve significant milestones, consider organizing a small celebration with your group. This could be a casual dinner, a fun outing, or even a virtual gathering where you can reflect on your journey so far. Use this time to share your individual experiences, the challenges you've faced, and the successes you've celebrated together. These gatherings can serve as powerful reminders of your collective commitment and the strength of your partnership, reinforcing the idea that you are not alone in this venture.

As you progress through the years, particularly as you reach the pivotal point of leveraging accumulated home equity, it's crucial to celebrate this new chapter in your investment journey. This strategy not only accelerates your property acquisition but also marks a significant shift in your financial capabilities. Celebrate the moment when you can use the equity from your first five properties to fund additional down payments. This achievement reflects not just your financial discipline but also the power of collaborative efforts in achieving your dreams.

Lastly, remember that success is not just about the end goal but also about the journey itself. Celebrate the daily habits you cultivate by saving $20 each day. These small yet impactful actions are the building blocks of your future success. Each time you set aside that amount, you are investing not just in property, but in your dreams and aspirations. By consistently recognizing and celebrating both the small victories and the larger achievements, you will create a positive environment that fosters growth, motivation, and an enduring commitment to your real estate investment journey.

Chapter 8

Growing Your Portfolio

Leveraging home equity

Leveraging Home Equity is a powerful strategy that can significantly enhance your real estate investment journey, especially for those just starting out. As you and your group of six individuals embark on your shared goal of saving $20 a day, your initial properties will not only provide rental income but also increase in value over time. This increase can be tapped into, allowing you to use the equity built within those properties to fuel further investments. Home equity is essentially the difference between what your property is worth and what you owe on your mortgage. By understanding how to access this equity, you can unlock new opportunities for growth in your rental portfolio.

As you reach the sixth year of your investment strategy, the equity accumulated in your first five properties will begin to play a pivotal role. For instance, if your rental properties appreciate in value, you could potentially access 70-80% of that increased equity through a home equity line of credit (HELOC) or a cash-out refinance. This means that the hard work and discipline you have put into saving and investing can now translate into significant funds that can be reinvested into additional down payments for new properties. It's an exciting transition that can feel like a financial booster shot for your group's ambitions.

The key to successfully leveraging home equity lies in careful planning and a clear understanding of your financial goals. As you pool your savings together, ensure that you are also maintaining a strong credit profile, as this will affect your ability to access equity. Open discussions among your group about financial responsibilities and strategies will build trust and enhance group dynamics. Keeping everyone informed and engaged in the decision-making process will not only strengthen your partnership but also lead to more informed choices regarding how much equity to tap into for your next investments.

Furthermore, leveraging home equity can lead to a compounding effect in your investment strategy. Each new property acquired will contribute additional rental income, which can further increase your savings. By strategically reinvesting the profits from your rental properties, you can create a cycle of growth that accelerates your ability to purchase more real estate. This cumulative approach will help you achieve your long-term goal of building a robust rental portfolio, providing financial security and potential wealth for everyone involved.

In conclusion, as you embark on this journey of collaborative real estate investment, remember that leveraging home equity is not just about accessing cash; it's about strategically using your existing investments to fuel future successes. Your commitment to saving and investing together will lay the foundation for a thriving portfolio. Embrace the power of home equity, stay focused on your goals, and enjoy the financial freedom that comes with smart real estate investing. Together, you can transform your daily savings into a legacy of property ownership that benefits all members of your group.

Scaling Your Investment Strategy

Scaling your investment strategy requires a clear vision and a commitment to collaboration. As you and your group of friends embark on this journey of saving $20 daily, it's essential to recognize the power of teamwork. By pooling your resources, you're not just saving money; you're building a foundation for significant financial growth. Each couple brings unique strengths to the table, whether it's financial planning, market research, or property management. Embrace these dynamics, as leveraging each other's skills will enhance your collective strategy and lead to successful investments.

As your savings accumulate, the first critical step is to establish a structured approach to property acquisition. With an annual goal of purchasing one or two rental properties, focus on setting clear timelines and benchmarks. The strategy of using 7% of the home price as a down payment simplifies the process, allowing everyone to visualize the path forward. Regularly revisit and adjust your goals based on your savings progress and market conditions. This adaptability will ensure that you stay on track and can capitalize on opportunities as they arise.

Once you have successfully acquired your initial properties, the next phase involves leveraging the equity gained from these investments. As you reach year six, you will notice the financial benefits of your hard work manifesting as increased home values and rental income. This equity can serve as a powerful tool for funding additional down payments, enabling you to scale your portfolio more quickly than you initially thought possible. Remember, each new property not only adds to your income but also strengthens your collective investment strategy.

To maintain momentum, it's vital to cultivate daily savings habits and encourage each other throughout the process. Celebrate small victories, such as achieving quarterly savings goals or securing a new property. Engaging in regular discussions about financial planning will keep everyone motivated and aligned in your vision. Sharing tips on savings techniques and exploring creative ways to increase your collective income can also enhance your investment strategy, making it a collaborative effort that reinforces your commitment.

Finally, remember that the journey of real estate investing is not just about financial gain but also about the bonds you create with one another. As couples, your shared experiences in navigating this path will foster deeper relationships and a supportive environment. Embrace the challenges and celebrate the successes together, knowing that you are building not just a rental portfolio but also a future filled with financial freedom and shared dreams. Scaling your investment strategy is not just a financial endeavor; it's a transformative journey that brings you closer together.

Strategies for Buying Multiple Properties

One of the most effective strategies for buying multiple properties is to start by establishing a solid savings habit. For the six committed individuals in your group, saving $20 a day may seem small, but over time, it accumulates into a significant amount. By pooling your resources, you can reach your financial goals faster. This daily savings routine not only builds discipline but also creates a sense of shared purpose among the group. Each couple can motivate one another, ensuring that everyone stays on track to reach the collective target. Celebrate small milestones together to keep the enthusiasm high and reinforce the commitment to your shared dream of property ownership.

As you accumulate savings, it's crucial to understand how to leverage them effectively. With a target home price of $200,000, aiming to save 7% for a down payment of $14,000 is a smart strategy. This approach allows you to secure your first property while minimizing financial risk. Collaborating with your partners can enhance your purchasing power. When considering investment opportunities, always evaluate properties that have the potential for appreciation and strong rental yields. This will ensure that your investments contribute positively to your income and allow you to reinvest in additional properties in the future.

Once you've successfully purchased your initial properties, focus on maintaining and managing them effectively. A well-maintained property not only maintains its value but can also generate consistent rental income. As your experience grows, consider taking on more responsibilities within the group, such as property management or tenant relations. Sharing these tasks can help distribute the workload and strengthen the bonds within your group. This collaborative approach will not only streamline operations but also foster a deeper understanding of the real estate market among all members.

By year six, you'll be in a prime position to leverage the equity built in your first properties for future acquisitions. This concept of using accumulated equity allows you to fund down payments for additional properties without significantly affecting your savings plan. As property values increase and your equity grows, your potential for expansion multiplies. Keep in mind that smart financial planning is essential; always assess your debt-to-income ratio and ensure that you are not over-leveraging. This careful approach will safeguard your investments and facilitate sustained growth in your property portfolio.

Lastly, remember that the journey of property investment is a marathon, not a sprint. The goal of acquiring multiple properties over the next 10 to 15 years requires patience, perseverance, and adaptability. Regularly revisit your goals, and adjust your strategies as necessary. The dynamic nature of the real estate market means you may need to pivot your approach based on changing conditions. Celebrate your successes along the way and learn from any setbacks. With dedication and teamwork, your group will not only achieve its aspirations but also create a lasting legacy of financial stability and growth through real estate investment.

Chapter 9

Long-Term Planning

Setting Goals for the Next 10-15 Years

Setting long-term goals is essential for any successful venture, and when it comes to building a rental property portfolio, having a clear vision for the next 10 to 15 years can significantly enhance your chances of success. For couples and groups of friends collaborating on real estate investment, setting specific, measurable, achievable, relevant, and time-bound (SMART) goals will help keep everyone aligned and motivated. With a shared commitment to saving $20 each day, you'll be building a solid foundation for your future investments. Think about what you want to achieve in this time frame, such as the number of properties to acquire or the total rental income to generate.

As you embark on this journey, it's crucial to define milestones that mark your progress. For instance, you might set a goal to purchase your first property by the end of year one, followed by one or two additional properties each subsequent year. By year six, when you begin to leverage the equity from your initial acquisitions, aim for a significant uptick in your property portfolio. These milestones will not only provide direction but also serve as motivation for you and your partners as you celebrate each achievement together.

Establishing a comprehensive financial plan is another vital aspect of setting your goals. Calculate the total amount you need to save over the years to meet your down payment requirements, considering your target home price of $200,000 and the 7% needed each year. This translates to approximately $14,000 annually for each couple or individual in your group. By keeping track of your savings and ensuring everyone contributes their fair share, you'll create a sense of accountability and teamwork, which is essential for long-term success.

In addition to financial goals, consider setting objectives related to learning and development. As you progress through the years, take time to educate yourselves about the rental market, property management, and investment strategies. Attend workshops, read books, and network with experienced investors to deepen your understanding of the industry. This knowledge will empower you to make informed decisions and adapt your strategies as needed, ensuring that you are well-prepared to navigate the challenges that may arise.

Finally, remember that flexibility is key in reaching your long-term goals. Life can bring unexpected changes, and your plans may need to evolve over time. Regularly review your goals and adjust them as necessary to reflect your current circumstances or market conditions. By maintaining an encouraging and proactive approach, you and your investment partners can remain focused on your vision while adapting to new opportunities that may arise along the way. Embrace the journey, and let each step forward bring you closer to your dream of a flourishing rental property portfolio.

Adapting Strategies Over Time

Adapting strategies over time is crucial for any group embarking on a collective investment journey. For the six individuals in our challenge, it's not just about saving $20 daily; it's about evolving their approach as circumstances change and as they grow in their understanding of real estate investment. As they begin this journey, they need to be open to reassessing their methods, learning from experiences, and adjusting their strategies to maximize their potential. This adaptability will be key in transforming their pooled savings into a thriving rental property portfolio.

In the initial years, the focus will be on establishing a solid foundation. Each couple must commit to their daily savings habit, ensuring that they consistently contribute toward their goal. They should regularly communicate about their progress and challenges, keeping the momentum alive. By sharing successes and setbacks, they can foster a supportive environment that encourages innovation. This collaborative spirit will be vital when they start to explore different property types and investment opportunities, allowing them to pivot their strategies based on what they learn from the market and each other.

As they approach year five and begin to acquire their first properties, the group will need to evaluate their investment strategies. They should analyze the performance of their initial rental properties and assess whether their current approach aligns with market trends. This could mean diversifying into different neighborhoods or property types, or even adjusting the amount they set aside for down payments. The experience gained from managing these properties will provide invaluable insights, enabling them to refine their strategies for future acquisitions.

When the group reaches year six, they'll have the added advantage of home equity from their first properties. This equity can be leveraged to fund additional down payments, effectively accelerating their investment strategy. As they adapt to using their accumulated wealth, it's important for them to stay informed about financial products that can help them optimize these opportunities. Collaborating with financial advisors or attending investment workshops can provide new perspectives and strategies, ensuring they make informed decisions that align with their long-term goals.

Ultimately, the journey of adapting strategies over time is about growth, both as individual investors and as a cohesive group. By remaining flexible and willing to learn, they can navigate the complexities of the real estate market while building a robust rental portfolio. The commitment to saving, open communication, and strategic planning will empower these couples to not only achieve their financial goals but also to cultivate a lasting partnership that thrives on shared success.

Evaluating and Adjusting Your Portfolio

Evaluating and adjusting your portfolio is a crucial step in ensuring that your group's investment strategies align with your long-term goals. As you embark on this journey of saving $20 a day and pooling your resources for property acquisitions, it's vital to regularly assess how your investments are performing. Begin by reviewing the rental yields of your properties and comparing them against market standards. This analysis will help you identify which properties are thriving and which may need more attention. Open communication within your group will foster a collaborative environment, allowing everyone to share insights and make informed decisions about any necessary adjustments.

As your group continues to save and invest, consider setting specific milestones to evaluate your progress. For instance, after acquiring your first few properties, take time to assess your overall financial health. Are your rental incomes meeting your expectations? Are there unforeseen expenses that could impact your savings plans? By maintaining transparency about your financial situation, you can collectively strategize on how to address any challenges, whether that means refinancing a property or increasing your monthly savings. Celebrating your achievements at each milestone will keep everyone motivated and focused on the shared vision.

Leveraging equity from your properties will become a powerful tool in your investment strategy, especially as you reach the six-year mark. By evaluating the accumulated equity, your group can make informed decisions about which properties to refinance or how to use that equity for down payments on new acquisitions. This approach not only accelerates the growth of your rental portfolio but also maximizes your investment potential. As you tap into this equity, ensure that you weigh the benefits against any associated risks, as responsible management will dictate the success of your future investments.

Adjusting your portfolio is not merely about the numbers; it's also about understanding the dynamics of your group. Each member brings unique perspectives and strengths to the table. Encourage open discussions about financial goals, risk tolerance, and investment strategies. This collaborative approach will enhance decision-making and foster a sense of ownership among all members. Remember that investing in real estate is a marathon, not a sprint. By nurturing a supportive environment, you'll be better equipped to navigate challenges and celebrate successes together.

Lastly, embrace the idea that evaluating and adjusting your portfolio is an ongoing process. The real estate market is dynamic, and your strategy must be adaptable to changing conditions. Regular check-ins, perhaps quarterly or biannually, will allow your group to stay aligned with your goals and make timely adjustments. As you continue to save and invest, remember that each decision you make today lays the foundation for your future success. Together, you are building not just a portfolio of properties, but a legacy of teamwork, financial literacy, and shared dreams.

Chapter 10

Financial Planning for Couples

Aligning Financial Goals as a Couple

Aligning financial goals as a couple is an essential step toward building a successful investment strategy, especially when you are embarking on a journey to create a rental property portfolio. Open communication is the cornerstone of this process. Start by discussing your individual financial aspirations, lifestyle preferences, and long-term visions. Understanding each other's motivations will help you create a shared financial picture. For instance, consider how much you both want to save, what types of properties interest you, and your timeline for achieving these goals. By aligning your visions, you can work together more effectively and maintain a strong partnership throughout your investment journey.

Once you've established your shared goals, it's time to set specific, measurable milestones. Commit to saving $20 a day, which might seem modest, but over time, it can lead to significant savings. Together, calculate how much you will have at the end of the year—about $14,600 for both of you combined. This amount can be earmarked for down payments on rental properties, which are typically around $14,000 for a $200,000 home. By breaking down your larger goal into smaller, achievable targets, you'll have a clearer path to follow, making it easier to stay motivated and engaged in your savings journey.

Creating a budget that reflects your joint financial priorities is crucial. This budget should accommodate your daily savings while also allowing for necessary expenses and some leisure activities. It's important to find a balance that doesn't feel restrictive but still prioritizes your goal of property acquisition. Use budgeting tools or apps that allow both of you to track your spending and savings. This transparency will foster accountability, ensuring that you both contribute to the shared goal and stay committed to your financial plans.

As you continue saving, consider ways to enhance your investment strategy collectively. Explore opportunities for leveraging accumulated equity from your initial properties. Starting in year six, using the equity from your first five homes can provide a significant boost to your investment capacity, allowing you to acquire additional properties more quickly. Discuss how to assess and manage risks associated with leveraging equity, ensuring that both partners are comfortable with the strategy. This collaborative approach not only strengthens your investment strategy but also deepens your partnership and trust.

Finally, celebrate your progress together. Regularly review your achievements and reflect on how far you've come since you started saving. Acknowledge each milestone, whether it's reaching a savings target or successfully acquiring a new property. Celebrating your successes will help maintain motivation and reinforce the importance of teamwork in your financial journey. As you align your financial goals and work together toward shared aspirations, you'll not only build a robust rental portfolio but also strengthen your relationship, making the journey enjoyable and rewarding.

Managing Joint Finances

Managing joint finances is essential for the success of your group's real estate investment journey. When six individuals, like three couples, commit to saving $20 a day each, it creates a solid foundation for pooling resources effectively. This collaborative approach not only maximizes the potential for significant savings but also fosters a sense of shared purpose. Establishing clear communication channels about financial roles and responsibilities will ensure that everyone is on the same page. Regular discussions about savings progress, budgeting, and financial goals will help keep the momentum alive and strengthen the commitment to the group's objectives.

To effectively manage joint finances, it's crucial to create a transparent system for tracking contributions and expenses. Consider setting up a shared digital platform or spreadsheet where all members can view and record daily savings. This transparency builds trust and accountability, essential elements for any successful partnership. Additionally, setting up a joint savings account specifically for your real estate investments can simplify the process of pooling funds and making down payments. This account can be monitored collectively, allowing everyone to see how far you've come toward your goal of purchasing rental properties.

As you save collectively, it's important to celebrate milestones along the way. Recognizing each accomplishment, whether it's reaching a savings target or successfully acquiring your first property, will boost morale and reinforce the commitment to the group's vision. Regularly scheduled meetings can serve as a platform to share successes, discuss challenges, and adjust plans as necessary. This not only strengthens the bond between group members but also cultivates a supportive environment where everyone feels valued and motivated to contribute.

When it comes time to make a purchase, having a clear strategy for the funds will enhance your decision-making process. With each couple contributing to the down payment of the chosen property, it's essential to agree on selection criteria based on individual preferences and group dynamics. This can include location, property type, and potential for rental income. By working collaboratively to evaluate options, you can leverage the diverse insights within the group, ensuring that each investment aligns with your collective goals.

As you progress and start leveraging the equity from your properties, it will be vital to revisit your financial strategies periodically. This will help you adapt to changing market conditions and group dynamics. Being flexible and open to new ideas will empower your group to seize opportunities as they arise. With consistent savings habits and a commitment to managing your joint finances effectively, you will not only grow your rental portfolio but also lay the groundwork for a successful long-term investment strategy. Embrace the journey together, and watch your dreams transform into reality!

Building Wealth Together

Building wealth together is not just a dream; it's a tangible goal that can be achieved through commitment, collaboration, and strategic planning. For young couples and individuals looking to enter the world of real estate investing, pooling resources can be a game-changer. By committing to save $20 each day, each member of a group of six individuals can accumulate significant funds over time. With dedication, these savings can transform into a substantial down payment, paving the way for the purchase of rental properties that generate passive income and long-term financial security.

Imagine this: after saving diligently for a year, each couple has contributed $7,300 to their collective fund. By pooling these resources, they can make a down payment of $14,600 on a rental property priced at $200,000. This collective effort not only makes the financial burden lighter but also fosters a sense of camaraderie and shared purpose among the group. As they continue to save, year after year, their ability to acquire more properties grows, creating a powerful momentum that can lead to a robust rental portfolio.

The beauty of this strategy lies in its simplicity and effectiveness. As each couple stays committed to their daily savings habits, they cultivate financial discipline that extends beyond real estate. This habit not only prepares them for property acquisition but also instills a mindset geared towards long-term financial planning. By consistently setting aside funds, they build a foundation that can support multiple investments, thus maximizing their potential for wealth creation together.

As the years pass, the group can leverage the equity built in their initial properties to accelerate their investment journey. Starting in year six, the accumulated equity becomes a powerful tool for making additional down payments. This strategy allows them to scale their investment efforts, enabling them to purchase one or two additional properties each year. The ripple effect of this approach amplifies their wealth-building potential, creating a cycle of growth that benefits everyone involved.

Ultimately, the journey of building wealth together through real estate is not just about acquiring properties; it's about fostering relationships, establishing trust, and collectively achieving financial goals. This collaborative approach empowers each individual and couple to support one another while navigating the complexities of real estate investment. By embracing daily savings habits and strategic planning, they lay the groundwork for a prosperous future, proving that together, they can achieve more than they ever could alone.

Chapter 11

Success Stories

Real Experiences from Our Group

In our journey as a group committed to saving $20 each day, we have encountered both challenges and triumphs that have shaped our collective experience. Each couple brought their unique financial backgrounds and perspectives, which enriched our discussions and strategies. Initially, we faced skepticism from friends and family who questioned our ability to save such a modest amount consistently. However, as we began to see our savings accumulate, our confidence grew. The simple act of setting aside $20 each day became a powerful daily ritual, reinforcing our commitment not just to our goals but to one another as well.

Our first year was both exciting and enlightening as we pooled our savings. The process of choosing our first property was a shared experience filled with debates and negotiations. We learned to communicate openly about our expectations and concerns, fostering an environment of trust and collaboration. This transparency not only strengthened our group dynamics, but it also allowed us to make informed decisions together. When we finally purchased our first rental property, the sense of accomplishment was palpable. We celebrated not just the acquisition, but the journey that got us there, embracing the lessons learned along the way.

As we moved into our second year, we decided to reinvest our rental income, which proved to be a game changer. The cash flow from our first property allowed us to maintain our daily savings habit while accelerating our down payment savings for the next house. We were amazed at how quickly our efforts compounded. By sharing tips on managing expenses and maximizing income, we discovered new savings techniques that worked for each couple's unique situation. This collaborative approach not only kept us motivated but also empowered us to think creatively about our financial strategies.

When we reached the sixth year, we were ready to leverage the equity built in our initial properties. This strategic move opened doors we hadn't anticipated, allowing us to purchase multiple properties in a single year. The excitement of witnessing our portfolio grow was a testament to the power of collective effort and strategic planning. As we shared our successes and challenges, we realized that our journey was not just about property acquisition but also about building a supportive community. Each couple had their own stories of perseverance, and these shared experiences fueled our motivation to keep pushing forward.

Looking ahead, our goal is to continue this journey for another decade, transforming our daily savings into a robust rental portfolio that will provide financial freedom for all of us. The commitment to save $20 a day has not only changed our financial landscape but has also forged lasting friendships and partnerships. By sharing our experiences, we hope to inspire other beginners to embark on similar journeys, proving that with dedication, collaboration, and a clear vision, anyone can turn their dreams of property ownership into reality. Together, we are excited about the future, and we invite you to join us on this transformative path.

Common Mistakes and How to Avoid Them

One of the most common mistakes beginners make when embarking on a property investment journey is underestimating the importance of consistent savings. Many individuals start with enthusiasm but fail to stick to their daily savings commitment of $20. This inconsistency can derail the entire plan, preventing them from pooling enough resources to make a meaningful down payment on a rental property. To avoid this pitfall, it's crucial to establish a routine and automate savings wherever possible. Setting up direct deposits or automatic transfers to a dedicated savings account can help ensure that the savings habit becomes a priority rather than an afterthought.

Another frequent error is neglecting to perform thorough research before diving into property purchases. Beginners might be tempted to rush into buying a property, driven by excitement rather than informed decision-making. This can lead to poor investments in locations that don't appreciate over time or properties that require excessive repairs. To steer clear of this mistake, it's essential to engage in comprehensive market analysis and understand factors like neighborhood trends, rental demand, and potential return on investment. Taking the time to educate yourselves will empower you to make informed choices that align with your long-term goals.

Collaboration can be both a strength and a challenge when investing as a group. Couples and friends pooling their resources may struggle with differing opinions on investment strategies or property choices. This can lead to conflicts that hinder progress. To mitigate this issue, establishing clear communication and setting shared goals from the outset is vital. Regular meetings to discuss financial updates, investment opportunities, and personal aspirations can help keep everyone on the same page and maintain a positive group dynamic. Agreeing on a decision-making process can prevent misunderstandings and foster a collaborative spirit.

Many newbie investors also fall into the trap of overlooking the financial implications of property ownership beyond the purchase price. Costs such as property taxes, maintenance, insurance, and potential vacancies can significantly impact the overall profitability of a rental property. To avoid being caught off guard, it's essential to create a comprehensive budget that includes all potential expenses. By doing so, you'll be better prepared to manage cash flow effectively and ensure that your rental properties remain profitable in the long run.

Finally, failing to consider the long-term vision can impede growth in a property investment strategy. New investors may focus solely on immediate gains without planning for future acquisitions or leveraging equity. This mindset can lead to stagnation rather than growth. To counter this, regularly revisit your investment goals and adjust your strategies accordingly. As you approach the six-year mark, begin to explore options for leveraging the equity built in your initial properties to fund additional acquisitions. By maintaining a forward-thinking perspective, you can continuously expand your rental portfolio and move closer to achieving your financial dreams.

Celebrating Milestones and Future Aspirations

Celebrating milestones is an essential part of any journey, especially when it comes to financial goals like purchasing rental properties. For our group of six committed individuals, each saving $20 a day, every year represents a significant step toward achieving our dream of building a robust rental portfolio. As we gather to reflect on our progress, we rejoice in the collective savings we've managed to amass, which is not just a number but a testament to our dedication and teamwork. Each year, as we pool our savings, we celebrate the purchase of our first home, marking a pivotal moment that validates our strategy and commitment. These milestones are reminders of what we can achieve together, motivating us to push forward.

As we look ahead, the future is bright with opportunities. With the goal of acquiring one or two properties every year, our strategy is designed to ensure that we not only grow our portfolio but also cultivate our financial literacy and investment acumen. Each property we acquire strengthens our foundation and enhances our ability to take calculated risks. By year six, we will begin to tap into the equity we have built from our initial purchases, allowing us to accelerate our growth. This strategic leveraging is a powerful tool that can exponentially increase our buying power and expand our horizons in the rental market.

The beauty of this journey lies in the collaborative effort we share as couples. Each member of our group brings unique perspectives and skills to the table, enriching our investment discussions and decision-making processes. The synergy we create fosters an environment where we can learn from one another, share insights, and innovate our strategies. Celebrating our milestones together not only strengthens our financial ties but also deepens our relationships, reminding us that we are not just investing in properties but also in each other.

As we celebrate our achievements, we also set our sights on the long-term vision we have for our rental portfolio. The commitment to save $20 a day may seem small, but when compounded over time, it carries immense potential. Our goal of owning multiple properties in 10 to 15 years is not just a dream; it is a tangible aspiration fueled by our daily habits and collective discipline. By adhering to our savings techniques and continuously refining our investment strategies, we are laying the groundwork for a prosperous future that benefits us all.

In essence, every milestone we celebrate is a stepping stone toward a future filled with possibilities. We acknowledge the hard work and sacrifices that come with our daily savings routines, understanding that these efforts are what will ultimately lead to financial independence and generational wealth. As we envision our future, we are excited about the prospects of expanding our rental portfolio and the financial freedom it will bring. Together, we will continue to celebrate our achievements while holding steadfast to our aspirations, knowing that each day brings us closer to realizing our dreams.

Chapter 12
Inspiring Others
Sharing Your Journey

Sharing your journey is an essential part of transforming your savings into property. For each of you, the commitment to save $20 daily may feel like a small step, but when combined with your partners, it transforms into a powerful force. Imagine that every day, you are not just setting aside money; you are building a future where financial independence and shared dreams come true. It's about creating a narrative together, where every dollar saved is a building block toward a collective goal. This journey will allow you to celebrate not just the milestones but also the small victories along the way.

As you embark on this adventure with your partners, sharing your experiences will deepen your bonds and keep everyone motivated. Celebrate the first month of savings, the first property purchase, and every moment in between. Use social media or a shared group chat to document your progress, exchange tips, and encourage each other when challenges arise. This openness fosters accountability and keeps everyone aligned with the vision of building a robust rental portfolio. Remember, each time you share your journey, you reinforce your commitment to the plan and inspire others to join in on the path to financial growth.

Consider the power of collaboration. Each couple brings unique skills and perspectives to the table, making your group dynamic a significant asset. One partner might excel at budgeting, while another may have a knack for negotiation or property management. By sharing these skills, you can enhance your collective knowledge and approach to real estate investment. Regular meetings to discuss progress, brainstorm ideas, and reassess strategies can keep your goals in focus. You are not just saving money; you are cultivating a shared vision and supporting each other in achieving it.

As your savings grow, so will your ability to leverage home equity for future investments. This strategy will become a critical part of your journey, especially as you reach the sixth year and beyond. By pooling your savings and utilizing the equity from your first properties, you will accelerate your purchase of additional homes. This is where the true magic happens—your initial commitment to save $20 daily multiplies, transforming into a powerful investment strategy that can yield returns beyond your expectations.

In the long run, the benefits of sharing your journey extend beyond financial gain. You'll develop resilience, teamwork, and a sense of accomplishment that comes from achieving a common goal. You are not just investing in properties; you are investing in your relationships and your futures. By embracing the journey together, you will create a legacy of financial literacy, collaboration, and empowerment that can inspire generations to come. So, embrace every moment, share your stories, and watch as your collective efforts lead to incredible transformations in your lives.

Building a Community of Savers

Building a community of savers is an essential step in transforming your financial future, especially for couples and individuals eager to venture into real estate investment. By committing to save $20 a day, you can create a powerful collective that not only supports individual goals but also amplifies your purchasing power. Imagine six individuals, or three couples, each dedicated to saving and investing together. This commitment transforms not just personal finance but also fosters a sense of community and shared purpose, motivating everyone to stay on track.

Pooling resources allows each member of the group to contribute towards a shared vision of property ownership. With the annual savings from each couple, you can collectively accumulate significant amounts that make a real impact. For instance, if each couple saves $20 a day, that amounts to $14,600 per year per couple. When combined, the group can save over $43,800 annually, a substantial amount that can be used for down payments on rental properties. This collective effort not only enhances the financial capacity of each member but also creates a support network that encourages accountability and shared learning.

As your group embarks on this journey, establishing clear goals and strategies is crucial. By adopting a strategic approach to property acquisition, you can use 7% of the home price, which is around $14,000 for a $200,000 property, as your down payment. This method allows your community to purchase one or two houses each year, setting the foundation for a robust rental portfolio. As you grow, the experience and knowledge shared within the group can lead to smarter investment decisions, helping everyone navigate the complexities of real estate.

In year six, the real magic happens as you leverage the accumulated home equity from your first five properties. This equity can serve as a powerful tool for your next down payments, allowing the group to acquire more properties without needing to save as much capital from scratch. This phase not only accelerates property acquisition but also reinforces the benefits of long-term planning and collaboration. By continuously reinvesting your gains, you build a sustainable model for wealth creation that can benefit all group members.

Ultimately, building a community of savers is about more than just financial gain; it's about fostering relationships and a shared vision for the future. Through collaborative real estate investment strategies, you learn from one another, celebrate successes together, and tackle challenges as a united front. The journey of saving and investing becomes a shared adventure that enriches both your financial lives and personal relationships, ensuring that your goals are not only achievable but also enjoyable. Embrace this journey together, and watch as your collective efforts lead to lasting financial empowerment.

Encouraging New Participants

Embarking on a journey of financial growth through real estate investment can seem daunting, especially for newcomers. However, the concept of pooling resources with like-minded individuals can transform this challenge into an exciting opportunity. Imagine six individuals, three couples, each committing to save just $20 a day. By collectively investing in real estate, not only do they make the process more manageable, but they also foster a supportive community that shares knowledge and encourages one another. This model is designed for those who are new to saving and investing, proving that with a little commitment and collaboration, significant financial milestones can be reached.

For each couple in this initiative, the power of teamwork plays a pivotal role. Saving $20 daily might seem small, but over a year, it accumulates to an impressive $14,600 when combined with the savings of their partners. This collective effort not only makes the goal of purchasing rental properties achievable but also cultivates an environment where couples can learn from each other's experiences. Sharing tips on budgeting, managing expenses, and staying motivated can help build a foundation of financial literacy that benefits everyone involved. Encouragement from peers can turn the daily act of saving into a rewarding journey rather than a mundane task.

As they strive toward their goal of acquiring rental properties, these couples will find that collaboration enhances their investment strategies. By pooling their resources, they can leverage their combined savings for down payments, allowing them to break into the real estate market sooner. With the aim of buying one or two houses each year, the couples can not only grow their individual wealth but also create a shared sense of accomplishment. This journey is not just about financial gain; it's about building relationships and fostering a spirit of collaboration that can lead to long-term success.

Once the initial properties are acquired, the strategy evolves. After five years of consistent saving and investment, the couples will be in a position to tap into the equity they've built in their properties. This equity can serve as a powerful tool for funding additional down payments, accelerating their property acquisition plan. The couples will discover that their efforts compound over time, creating a snowball effect that leads to even greater opportunities. This forward-thinking approach not only enhances their financial portfolios but also instills a sense of confidence and accomplishment in their investment journey.

Ultimately, the goal of creating a robust rental portfolio is within reach for these couples. By encouraging new participants to join this collaborative effort, they can help others realize that the path to financial freedom is accessible and rewarding. Each day of saving becomes a step toward achieving their dreams of property ownership, and the shared experiences will enrich their lives in ways they may not have anticipated. With mutual support, effective savings techniques, and a commitment to long-term planning, these couples are well on their way to transforming their savings into a legacy of real estate success.

Chapter 13

The Future of Real Estate

Trends in the Real Estate Market

The real estate market is constantly evolving, and understanding its current trends can significantly impact your investment journey. For young investors and couples embarking on the exciting path of property acquisition, keeping an eye on these trends is essential. One notable trend is the increasing popularity of collaborative investments. As more individuals recognize the power of pooling resources, your group of six can leverage this trend to maximize your purchasing power. By committing to save $20 a day, the combined savings can create a substantial financial foundation, allowing you to enter the market more confidently.

Another trend shaping the real estate landscape is the shift towards rental properties. With homeownership becoming increasingly challenging for many, the demand for rental units is on the rise. As you work together to acquire properties, focusing on the rental market can offer a steady income stream. This aligns perfectly with your strategy of using annual savings to make down payments on properties. By targeting areas with strong rental demand, you can ensure that your investments generate consistent cash flow, allowing you to reinvest in more properties over time.

Technology is also transforming the real estate market, making it easier than ever for newcomers to participate. Online platforms provide access to market data, property listings, and even crowdfunding opportunities. Embracing these digital tools can enhance your investment strategy, enabling you to identify promising neighborhoods and analyze property values effectively. By staying informed and utilizing technology, your group can make savvy investment decisions that align with your long-term goals.

Moreover, the focus on sustainable and eco-friendly housing is gaining momentum. As society shifts towards more environmentally conscious living, properties that emphasize sustainability are becoming more desirable. This trend is not only beneficial for the planet but can also increase the value of your investments. When selecting properties, consider those with energy-efficient features or green certifications, as they may attract higher-quality tenants and command better rental prices.

Finally, the importance of financial planning cannot be overstated in your investment journey. Establishing a clear plan that outlines your goals and timelines will help you stay focused and motivated. Incorporating regular discussions about finances within your group will strengthen your collaborative dynamic and ensure everyone is aligned. As you navigate the ups and downs of the real estate market, having a solid financial strategy will empower you to seize opportunities and overcome challenges, ultimately leading to a successful rental property portfolio over the next decade.

Innovations in Property Investment

Innovations in property investment have opened new avenues for individuals and couples looking to build wealth through real estate. For the six individuals committed to saving $20 daily, this innovative approach not only fosters a culture of saving but also aligns their financial goals with collective action. By pooling their resources, they can effectively leverage their combined savings to enter the real estate market, making property investment accessible even for those who might feel daunted by the initial costs. This group dynamic is crucial, as it encourages accountability and motivation among members, creating a supportive environment for all.

The strategy of saving $20 a day can seem small, but over time, it accumulates into significant capital. Each member contributes $7,300 annually, leading to a total of $43,800 for the group in the first year alone. This amount serves as a substantial down payment for their first property, reinforcing the idea that consistent, small contributions can lead to major financial breakthroughs. As they aim for properties valued at $200,000, the down payment of 7% enables them to secure their first rental home, laying the groundwork for a sustainable investment portfolio. This initial success builds confidence and enthusiasm, paving the way for future investments.

Once they have acquired their initial properties, the group can explore leveraging home equity to finance additional acquisitions. By year six, the accumulated equity from their first five properties can be used to fund new down payments, allowing them to expand their portfolio more rapidly. This innovative strategy not only increases the number of properties they own but also enhances their potential for cash flow and appreciation. Understanding and utilizing home equity is a key innovation that can significantly accelerate their journey toward financial independence and wealth creation.

Moreover, the collaborative approach to real estate investment fosters strong relationships among the couples involved. Sharing the responsibilities of property management, financing decisions, and market research not only lightens the load but also allows each member to leverage their unique skills and insights. This collaboration is instrumental in mitigating risks, as diverse perspectives can lead to better decision-making. By working together, they can navigate the challenges of property investment with more confidence and resilience, making the journey enjoyable and educational for everyone involved.

Ultimately, the goal of building a robust rental portfolio is attainable through innovative savings techniques and strategic planning. By committing to a daily savings habit, leveraging home equity, and collaborating effectively, these couples can create a lasting impact on their financial futures. This journey encourages not just financial discipline but also a sense of community, reminding them that they are not alone in their ambitions. As they continue this transformative process, they will not only achieve their property investment goals but also inspire others to embark on similar paths toward financial empowerment and growth.

The Next Generation of Investors

The next generation of investors is stepping onto the financial stage with a fresh perspective and a collaborative spirit. Gone are the days when individuals took on the daunting task of investing alone. Today, young couples are embracing the power of teamwork, pooling their resources to turn the dream of property ownership into reality. By committing to save just $20 a day, each individual contributes to a collective goal that not only fosters financial discipline but also strengthens relationships. This approach not only encourages consistent saving but also builds a robust foundation for long-term investment strategies.

Imagine the power of six individuals—three couples—who decide to embark on this investment journey together. Each couple commits to saving $20 daily, resulting in an impressive annual pool of savings. With an initial target of purchasing rental properties worth $200,000, they aim to leverage 7% of the home price as a down payment each year. This strategy not only makes real estate more accessible but also instills a sense of camaraderie among the couples. They celebrate each milestone together, reinforcing their commitment to financial growth and shared success.

As they navigate their investment journey, these couples will learn valuable lessons about financial planning and the importance of long-term vision. With a clear plan to acquire one or two properties each year, they will experience the thrill of building a diversified real estate portfolio. This gradual approach allows them to understand the intricacies of rental property management while also enjoying the benefits of passive income. By focusing on consistent savings and collaboration, they empower themselves to make informed decisions that will serve them well for years to come.

In years to come, as they reach the sixth year of their investment strategy, the couples will be in an even stronger position. With five properties under their belt, they will begin to leverage the equity accumulated in these homes to fund additional down payments. This strategic move will accelerate their property acquisition process, allowing them to grow their portfolio at an impressive pace. This not only reinforces the power of patience and persistence but also demonstrates how smart financial planning can lead to exponential growth.

Ultimately, the journey of these next-generation investors is a testament to the strength of collaboration and the benefits of a disciplined savings habit. By working together, they are not only transforming their financial futures but also creating a supportive network that fosters growth and resilience. This journey into property investment is not just about purchasing homes; it's about building a legacy of financial empowerment that will inspire others to follow suit. With commitment and teamwork, the sky is the limit for these aspiring investors, paving the way for a new era of real estate investment.

Chapter 14

Summary, Evaluation, Assessment & Reflection

Summary

1. This analysis presents a 10,15, 20-year projection of a real estate investment strategy undertaken by a group of 6 individuals each saving $20 a day.

2. The strategy focuses on annual property acquisition, cash flow generation from rental income, and compounding wealth through home appreciation.

3. The projections compare two approaches: a conservative strategy acquiring fewer properties annually and an aggressive strategy that scales faster by leveraging equity and reinvesting aggressively.

Evaluation

1. Across all key metrics—homes acquired, annual cash flow, and net worth—the aggressive strategy significantly outperformed the conservative approach.

2. While the conservative strategy showed steady growth and stability, the aggressive plan leveraged equity and reinvestment to generate exponential financial returns.

Assessment

1. The projections validate the effectiveness of consistent investing and the powerful impact of compounding in real estate.

2. Despite requiring greater risk tolerance, the aggressive strategy is a potent wealth-builder when combined with discipline and reinvestment.

3. Both strategies highlight how even modest daily savings can lead to substantial long-term financial independence.

Implications

1. Compounding real estate equity over time can create extraordinary wealth.

2. Small, consistent investments are accessible to most and deliver large rewards over decades.

3. Smart leverage and equity reinvestment are keys to accelerating portfolio growth.

4. Financial discipline, not income level, is the main differentiator in wealth building.

Reflection

1. This investment plan is a powerful example of how ordinary people can achieve extraordinary wealth.

2. It demonstrates that financial independence is not reserved for the wealthy but available to anyone willing to follow a smart, disciplined, and patient approach.

3. When grounded in faith and wise stewardship, these principles provide both financial and spiritual empowerment.

4. This model offers a pathway to break generational poverty and build lasting legacy wealth.

Chapter 15

Real Estate Investment Growth Projections

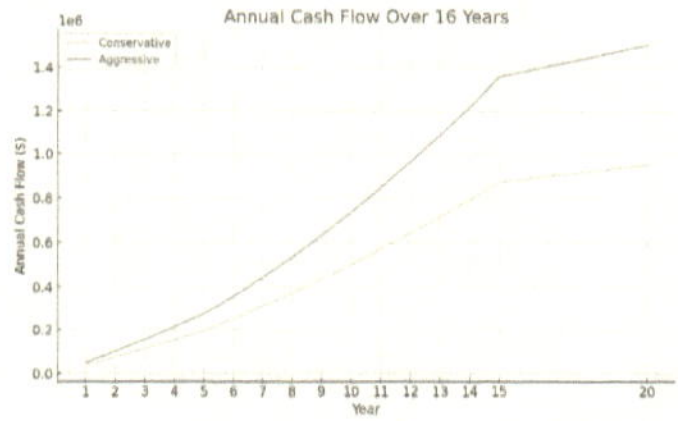

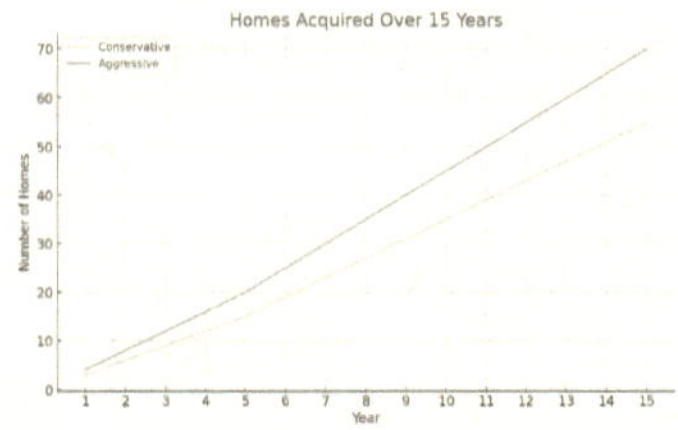

Graph showing Trend of Home Acquisition After 15 years

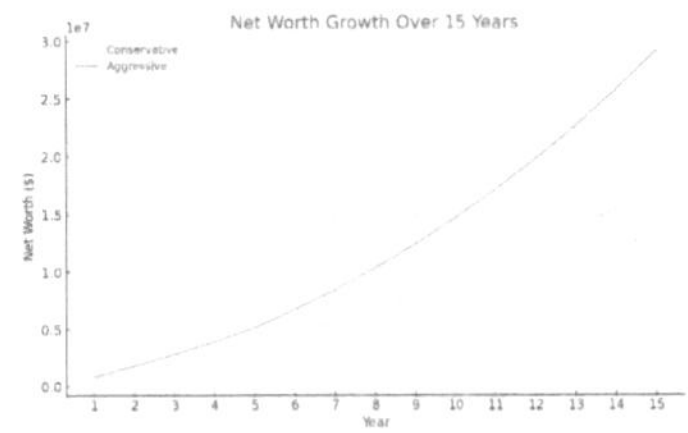

Trend of Networth After 15 years of Real Estate Investment

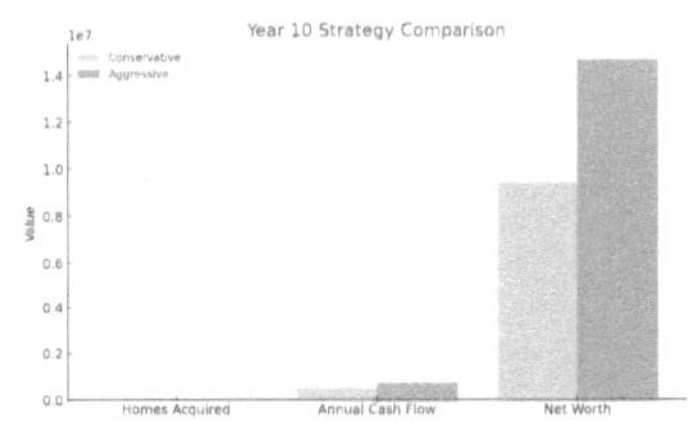

Graph Showing Total Number of Homes Acquired, Annual Cash Flow and Net worth

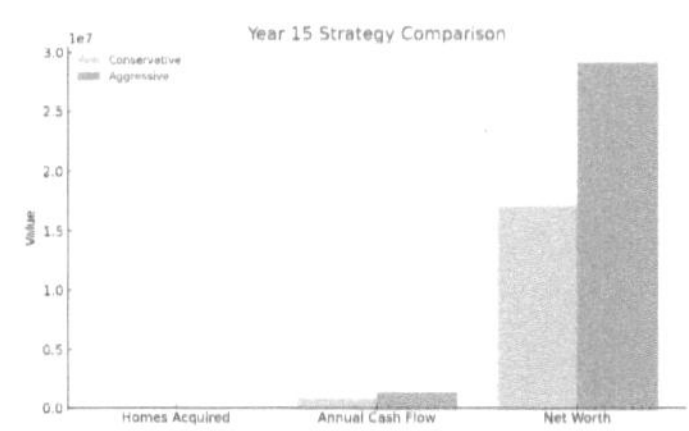

Graph of Homes Acquired, Annual Cash Flow and Net worth at Year 15

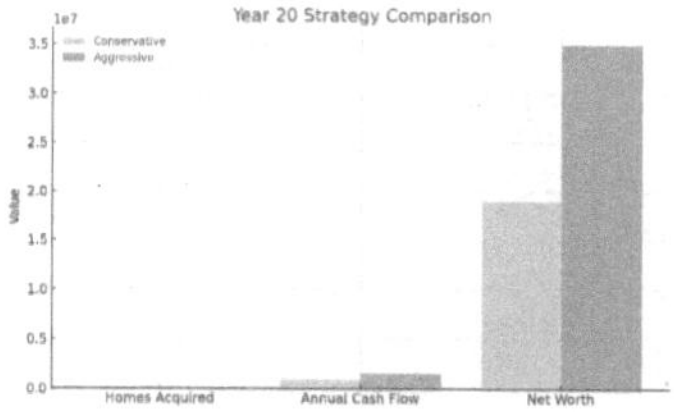

Graph of Homes Acquired, Annual Cash Flow and Net worth at Year 20

This report illustrates a 20-year real estate investment strategy executed by a group of six individuals saving $20 per day each. The goal is to use the savings and accumulated home equity to acquire rental properties, generating rental income and building net worth through appreciation and reinvestment.

www.ingramcontent.com/pod-product-compliance
Lightning Source LLC
LaVergne TN
LVHW090427210926
848480LV00002B/721
* 9 7 9 8 3 4 9 3 2 7 2 1 6 *